If Yo
My Family,
You'd Understand

A Family Systems Primer

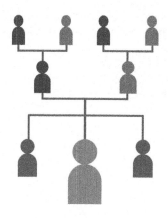

JACK SHITAMA

Charis Works

If You Met My Family, You'd Understand

© 2020 by Jack Shitama

Published by Charis Works, Inc. Earleville, Maryland. Inquiries may be sent to info@christian-leaders.com.

Edited by Trinity McFadden
Book cover design by Claire Purnell Graphic Design
Interior book design by Catherine Williams, Chapter One Book
    Production

ISBN 978-1-7320093-6-3 (Paperback)
ISBN 978-1-7320093-9-4 (Ebook)

Also by Jack Shitama

Anxious Church, Anxious People: How to Lead Change
in an Age of Anxiety

One New Habit, One Big Goal: Change Your Life in 10 Weeks

With Teryl Cartwright

Anxious Church, Anxious People: How to Lead Change
in an Age of Anxiety Companion Workbook

Table of Contents

Introduction

This book is about what I've learned over the years using family systems theory as a lens for learning how to be a non-anxious presence. Whether it's raising children, caring for a parent, relating to siblings, or any of the other numerous ways you function in your family of origin, this kind of presence has a life-giving impact that is hard to overstate. Presence matters. *Your* presence matters.

The title is humorous, but a bit misleading. A more accurate title would be, *"Now That I Understand My Family, I Better Understand Myself"*. This is not so you can blame your family for how you function. It's exactly the opposite. It's so you can more effectively take responsibility for yourself and how you function.

There is somebody in your family who makes you anxious. Maybe more than one person. When you see a text message, voicemail, or email from them, your anxiety skyrockets. This book will help you to get a different perspective on that (or those) relationship(s). Rather than blaming or diagnosing, it will help you to see things from a systems perspective. It will give you some distance to see that the only thing you can change is yourself—but that change can make all the difference in the world.

I wrote my first book, *Anxious Church, Anxious People: How to Lead Change in an Age of Anxiety*, to help church leaders apply family systems theory to congregational systems. I was especially interested in helping those who were working with churches that were stuck or dying. One of the primary principles in the book was that if you deal with the unresolved anxiety in your family of origin, it will make you a better leader. This approach necessarily required applying family systems principles to oneself, regardless of one's leadership context.

What I found was that people found it as helpful personally as they did professionally. One clergy colleague said to me, "I found this book so helpful, especially with my wife." This comment, as well as that of others, made me realize that a book about stuck congregations could help people function in healthier ways in their personal relationships.

After the book came out, my wife kept telling me that I needed to write a general family systems primer. Every family has its dysfunctions and struggles with anxiety. Some do to a lesser extent, but nobody gets the problem they can handle (more on that later).

Of course, being the good husband that I am, I ignored her advice. I had a book in my head about habit formation, then I collaborated with a curriculum writer to do a companion workbook for the first book. But, being the good husband that I am, I eventually listened to my wife. So, this is that book. If you've tried to read about family systems before, you may have gotten stuck on a lot of dense and academic language. I've tried to make family systems theory easily understood through plain language and simple examples. I hope you find it helpful. If you're ready to work on that, then let's get started.

One note: I write regular articles on family systems theory and leadership. You can find out more at www.thenonanxiousleader.com.

Chapter 1

The Symmetry of Life

The drool spot on my right shoulder got me thinking.

It was there most days.

Some days it was from my five-month-old grandson, Thomas. He's our first. Before he was born, people kept saying, "Oh, being a grandparent is the best! There's nothing like it!"

Because of the buildup, when people would ask me if I was excited to be a grandpa. I would always say yes. In my mind I was thinking, "This better be good!"

And, of course, it is.

I get to see Thomas several days a week. At that young age, I tried to hold him as much as possible. When I did, he would drool on my right shoulder. I'd gotten used to checking to see if I needed to clean off my shoulder, but sometimes I'd get to the end of the day and there it was. It made me smile.

Other days the drool spot came from my father-in-law. He had a debilitating stroke that paralyzed his right side, made his speech unintelligible, and left him with a condition called dysphagia, which means he has difficulty swallowing. We take part in his care and, because of the dysphagia, I would usually get a drool spot on my right shoulder as I would transfer him in and out of his wheelchair.

My father-in-law goes by Tom, and Thomas, his first great-grandchild, is his namesake.

Symmetry.

The drool spot got me thinking about how precious life is and how we shouldn't take anything for granted. I'm sure this is not new to you. It's not new to me. But thinking about Tom and Thomas has deepened my appreciation. (Although maybe I'm just getting old.)

Here's what I've learned.

Accept the Things You Cannot Change

Tom's stroke came two months after his seventy-eighth birthday. He was in great shape. Just before his birthday, he and eleven of his buddies made a golf trip to Ireland. He played seven courses in seven days and walked every one of them.

Tom coached high school and college football in Delaware, and it seems that he knows everyone in the state. The outpouring of love that came after his stroke was overwhelming, especially from his former players. He had made an impact on their lives.

The sentiment at the time was that it was tragic that this stroke had damaged his body so severely in his golden years.

I guess that's still true, but these years with him have given me a different perspective. I believe everybody has their time to go be with God, and it wasn't Tom's time.

That doesn't make it easy. And ours isn't the only family that has to deal with challenging circumstances. In fact, I think most families have challenges that make life hard.

But as a camp staff member said one summer, just because it's hard, doesn't mean it's not good. Tom is still with us, and I am grateful. It's hard, but it is still good to have him.

The Serenity Prayer by Reinhold Niebuhr puts it best:

> God, grant me the serenity to accept the things I cannot change, Courage to change the things I can, And wisdom to know the difference.

Being Is More Important Than Doing

I'm not a Type A personality, but I am a doer. I like to keep busy and to get things done. Once, my wife, Jodi, and I were on the planning team for a national camp and retreat event. We arrived at the venue two days before to get ready, helped run the four-day event, and then spent a whole day afterward debriefing. It was nonstop activity for a week. We had decided to relax that weekend at a nearby hotel with a nice water view, before traveling home.

The first day there I spent about six hours straight just sitting in an Adirondack chair on the deck, looking at the water. I didn't read. I didn't get my laptop out. I just sat. I was so whipped from the previous week that I just needed to do nothing. Jodi kept asking me if I was OK. She wasn't used to seeing me do nothing, so she was worried. Like I said, I'm not Type A, but it made me laugh that she was concerned about my lack of activity.

When Thomas was an infant, I just wanted to hold him. I didn't even talk to him that much. I probably should have, to help develop his verbal skills. But I just liked to hold him.

One day I was holding him, and I realized how different this was than when I was parenting our four kids. I love them and loved holding them. But I recognized the difference. As a parent, when I was holding my child, all I could think about were all the things that I had to get done. Work, household chores, etc. The classic conundrum was when a child went to sleep, should I take a nap because I was dead tired, or should I get something done because I could? It was usually the latter.

Holding Thomas is different. When I'm holding him, I don't think about what else I need to do. I enjoy the time we have. Perhaps this is age, wisdom, life experience, or some combination of the three. But I hadn't learned this lesson until now. Being is more important than doing. We are human beings, not human doings.

There is something in me that says I could not have learned these lessons before now. Perhaps that's true. And maybe the reason I share this is so I can remind myself to be grateful for what Tom and Thomas have taught me.

The Paradox of Family

Families can be our biggest joy and our greatest source of stress. Without a healthy connection to family, we can feel isolated and alone. But if we are too close, we can feel smothered.

You purchased this book for a reason. Whether you can't stand your family or can't stand to be without them, you have decided you want to figure out a better way. Like my experience with Tom and Thomas, it doesn't matter how long it's taken you to get to this point. Life's symmetry has brought you here. You have taken that step toward healthier functioning. The first step is to recognize the difference between a problem and a challenge.

Questions for Reflection:

What do you value about your family of origin?

What makes you anxious?

What has your life experience taught you about what you can and can't change?

Chapter 2

Problem and Challenge

"Nobody gets the problem they can handle."

Edwin Friedman

There is a difference between a challenge and a problem. A challenge is something difficult: an obstacle, a disruption, a situation that needs to be addressed or things could get worse. A problem is a challenge that causes so much anxiety that it becomes too difficult to handle. It is this anxious response to a challenge that turns it into a problem; we make it even more difficult to address because of our anxiety.

Like many children, our grandson experienced separation anxiety when he started going to daycare. So did we. He was about fourteen months old, which is in the age range when separation anxiety peaks.

The phenomenon is the result of children developing what is called object permanence. This is the idea that you know something exists even if you can't see it. For example,

11

if you place a toy under a blanket, a child with object permanence will know it's there and will try to find it.

Prior to developing object permanence, children are fine with just about anyone caring for them. But once they have this conception, they realize when their parent or primary caregiver is not with them, and this creates anxiety.

When Thomas started going to daycare, he would cry when he was dropped off. The daycare provider said that he would only cry for a few minutes, and then he was fine. But that doesn't really help the parent (or grandparent), who worries about whether he really is fine. The question was: Would this be a problem, or a challenge?

Nobody gets the problem they can handle, because if they could handle it, it wouldn't be a problem. More often than not, it's how we address a challenge that turns it into a problem.

My daughter and son-in-law have developed a routine with our grandson. This includes time spent with each parent, and then they will say, "Let's talk about our day." Then they will tell him that they're going to work and that he's going to daycare.

This is counterintuitive. It might seem easier to avoid upsetting him by just taking him to daycare without telling him. But this approach can actually make things worse.

In the first few weeks, their mornings were a mess. Thomas doesn't go to daycare every day, so perhaps he was anxious about what was happening. Telling him if he is going to daycare not only helps him to face reality, but it also removes the uncertainty that can create unnecessary anxiety.

You cannot avoid a challenge or help others avoid it. The best thing you can do is face it as a non-anxious presence.

Anxiety Is Poison

According to Seth Godin, non-clinical anxiety is experiencing failure in advance. Anxiety makes any situation worse. This is what turns a challenge into a problem. In any system, whether family, congregation, or organization, anxiety will make it harder for people to function at their best. This means we need to learn to deal with our own anxiety, as well that of others, to keep a challenge from becoming a problem.

If you read articles for parents on separation anxiety, it advises against sneaking out the door when dropping off a child at daycare. Doing this actually makes it harder for the child once she realizes the adult is gone. It's better to actually say goodbye, while being a non-anxious presence.

Sometimes we think we are making it easier for others, when we are actually making it harder. But what we are doing is sparing ourselves the pain of watching someone else struggle. Instead of allowing somebody to face their challenge, we are creating a problem. This often comes from being unwilling to deal with our own anxiety. Be aware of how you are avoiding a challenge, and whether this is making it worse (creating a problem), rather than helping.

One way to deal with anxiety is to keep it light.

Children, just like pets and other adults, can sense our anxiety. Keeping our attitude light and playful can help prevent our own anxiety from making things worse.

This is definitely an example of "fake it until you make it." You may still feel anxious, but you are able to regulate that anxiety, so it doesn't turn a challenging situation into a problem.

You might even try a little humor. This is a way to regulate your own anxiety to keep it from making a challenge into a problem.

A couple weeks into Thomas' separation anxiety, things improved. One day, his parents told him he was going to daycare. He wanted to snuggle. But he didn't cry. He dealt with it. And when they dropped him off, he took off his hat and coat and gave them to his caregiver. He's learning to face a challenge. So can we.

The Need to Be Right

One of the ways we turn a challenge into a problem comes from our need to be right. There is a difference between knowing what you believe and the need to have others agree with you. The need to be right creates anxiety. Have you ever had an argument with someone because the fact that they disagreed with you made you anxious, even angry? This is how a challenge becomes a problem.

The fact that you disagree with someone is not a problem. Disagreements occur all the time. But you don't have to be disagreeable. If you are not able to say what you believe, while giving others the freedom to disagree, then you have a problem. And the problem is of your own making.

Let me be clear. In some situations, others may disagree. That doesn't mean you have to agree with them. The question is whether you will let your own anxiety make the situation worse.

For example, your seventh-grade daughter wants to go to a high school party with her friends. You say no. She throws a tantrum and says she hates you. What do you do? You can respond with your own yelling and screaming. You can lay out all the reasons why you are right and she is wrong. Neither is likely to work. Have you ever tried to convince a teenager of anything? To the extent your own anxiety is unleashed, the situation will get worse—so let her disagree.

But there is a difference between giving someone the freedom to disagree and giving in. In this case, you know you are right. But that doesn't mean you need to convince your daughter. Keep your anxiety in check. Remain a non-anxious presence. Whether or not she agrees with you is not important. What's important is to prevent your anxiety from poisoning the situation through a reaction of yelling and screaming. You can say, "Honey, I know you think it's OK. But I disagree. And it's my job to look out for you. I love you, and I'm not allowing you to go." If you can do this in your best non-anxious presence, having her agree is not important.

You should be able to translate this situation to a congregation or organization. You know what you believe. Can you express it in healthy ways? What do you do in the face of others' anxiety? Do you feel the need to be right? Do you just give in without expressing your own opinion?

Effective leaders are able to express what they believe while giving others the freedom to disagree. This requires self-differentiation.

Self-Differentiation

A self-differentiated person is someone who is able to act according to her own values, while staying emotionally connected to others in the system, even when there is pressure to conform to the values of the system. It is the foundational concept in family systems theory. Developed by Murray Bowen in the 1960s, it is a theory of interdependence that teaches we don't act independently of our family of origin. Bowen believed that the most one could expect to act in self-differentiated ways was 70 percent of the time. And most of us do so less than 50 percent.

I encountered family systems theory in my first year of seminary. It changed my life. It helps me understand who I am as a person and how to function in healthy ways in my family of origin, in my church, and in the ministry I serve. Edwin H. Friedman, in his book *Generation to Generation: Family Process in Church and Synagogue*, defines self-differentiation as "The capacity of a family member to define his or her own life's goals and values apart from surrounding togetherness pressures."[1] Let's break that down.

Every system has its own way of doing things. It affects

every aspect of life. There are unwritten (and sometimes written) rules that define how we are to act and how we respond to virtually every situation. These unwritten rules create surrounding togetherness pressure. When somebody in the system goes against the rules, even for a good reason, it can create tension and anxiety, resulting in surrounding togetherness pressure. I find the easiest way to explain surrounding togetherness pressure is through the example of how families handle holidays.

When I was growing up, we were one of the first families to have a fake Christmas tree. Back then, a fake tree had no resemblance to the real thing. Every December, my dad would haul down the tree from the attic and we would assemble it, usually about three weeks before Christmas. As presents arrived in the mail from various relatives they would end up under the tree. As we got closer to Christmas, the number of presents grew, as did our excitement. We would go to bed on Christmas Eve, and when we awoke, Santa had delivered presents for all of us.

Oddly, my best friend across the street, Jamie, had a different family tradition. They wouldn't even buy a tree until about a week before Christmas. They didn't set it up. It sat leaning against the back of their house. They would go to bed on Christmas Eve, and, while they were sleeping, "Santa" would set up their tree, decorate it, and deliver all their presents. As a child, I used to wonder why Santa had so much more time for Jamie's family than for mine.

Which tradition was correct? Neither, of course. They were just different. But imagine if my friend's family tried to get a fake tree. I'm guessing there would be some significant surrounding togetherness pressure that would resist such a change.

Surrounding togetherness pressure is the pressure to conform. It creates, sustains and reinforces family norms. This became apparent to me when I went to my future in-laws' house for the first time for New Year's dinner. Coming from Pennsylvania, their traditional New Year's dinner was pork and sauerkraut. Food was being passed around. The mashed potatoes came first, then came the sauerkraut. I watched my (now) wife put a big spoonful of sauerkraut directly onto her mashed potatoes. I looked at her and exclaimed, "Who puts sauerkraut on top of their mashed potatoes?" Her entire family looked at me like I was from Mars. They said, "*We* do."

Whether we are dealing with a partner, congregant, or family member, surrounding togetherness pressure makes it difficult to express how we truly feel if we are not in agreement with the norms of the system. The ability to self-define in non-anxious ways when there is pressure to conform is the essence of self-differentiation.

The Non-Anxious Presence

Self-differentiation manifests itself in the ability to be a non-anxious presence, especially when there is surrounding togetherness pressure. This doesn't mean you don't feel anxious inside; it just means that you are able to regulate it in a way that doesn't poison the system.

To understand a non-anxious presence, it is helpful to know what it is not. It is *not* a non-anxious non-presence. It's easy to be non-anxious when you are not emotionally connected. It's easy to let things roll off your back when you don't really care. This is my default mode. I've gotten better at this over the years. My wife and I realized a long time ago that she would worry less if I would worry more. This didn't mean that I would have to be anxious, but it meant that I needed to engage emotionally in a way that showed I cared.

It is also *not* an anxious presence. This is someone who is so emotionally connected that she is unable to keep her own anxiety about another's functioning in check. An anxious presence tends to overfunction anxiously in the emotional space of others.

I can also be an anxious presence. Two of my children are heavy sleepers just like me. One of the things I've learned about parenting is the things that annoy us most about our children are the things that most resemble us. There was a pattern to my morning interactions with my heavy sleeping children when they were in high school. I would wake them repeatedly, and they would fall back to sleep. By the time bus arrival got near, I would feel very anxious and start yelling. This likely made them feel less motivated to actually get up. They often would miss the bus, and I would drive them to school, seething all the way. The irony of this is that this same pattern occurred between my dad and me when I was growing up (although my dad seemed to keep his anger in check).

Because a non-anxious presence is self-differentiated, she knows what she believes, but she doesn't require others to agree with her. Further, because she knows what she believes, she does not allow others to define her. And she is connected emotionally, but not so much so that any anxiety she does have becomes a problem.

How are you doing as a non-anxious presence?

Questions for Reflection:

When has your response turned a challenge into a problem? What could you have done differently?

Where do you experience surrounding togetherness pressure? How do you handle it?

To what extent are you able to express what you believe, while giving others the freedom to disagree? In what circumstances are you not able to do this?

Chapter 3

All Change Is Loss

"People aren't afraid of change, they're afraid of loss."
Sanford Shugart

By definition, all change is loss. The new reality means the old reality is gone. This is true when we think of traditional losses such as death, divorce, and unemployment. It's also true for positive changes such as marriage, birth, and promotion. Marriage is the end of one's single life. If you don't think birth changes everything, you haven't had to buy all the gear that comes with raising a child. A new job means the loss of the old. All change is loss. And with loss comes grief.

I believe the biggest challenge we face as individuals, families, and organizations is dealing with grief. But challenge is also an opportunity for growth. When we are honest about grief, we increase our ability to act in self-differentiated ways.

A Growth Opportunity

According to the American Psychological Association (APA), "Resilience is the process of adapting well in the face of adversity, trauma, tragedy, threats or significant sources of stress—such as family and relationship problems, serious health problems or workplace and financial stressors. It means 'bouncing back' from difficult experiences."[2] The APA emphasizes that resilience is not extraordinary; it is developed through one's response to adversity. Everyone experiences adversity. There is no way out or around it. The only way is through.

"No pain, no gain" is an idea most often associated with athletics or fitness. This is true of emotional health as well. If all change is loss, and loss involves grief, then the path to emotional well-being is directly through pain. Loss is painful, but it creates a growth opportunity. I had a mentor who was widowed suddenly at age seventy. When I would ask him how he was doing, he would say, "I am leaning into the pain." I think this sums up the opportunity perfectly. We don't often ask for it, but we can make the most of it.

Muscle growth is a great analogy for emotional growth. To get stronger, one must stress the muscles enough to create minor damage to them. The body repairs the muscles during periods of rest, making them stronger. When we deal with change directly, the resulting stress creates a growth opportunity. If we don't avoid it or deny it, but instead face it head on, we can increase resilience. This gives us a greater capacity to deal with adversity, change, and loss in the future.

Pain and Responsibility

To the extent that you are willing to lean into the pain of loss, you will grow in your capacity to endure emotional pain in the future. So just as an athlete builds capacity for physical pain, you can build the capacity for emotional pain.

Why is this important? As mentioned, this increases resilience. This will help you to better deal with your own anxiety and the anxiety in the systems in which you function. It will also increase your ability to deal with the pain of others.

This is key. It is actually our inability to withstand the pain of others that causes problems in our family of origin, congregation, or organization. Edwin Friedman writes in *Generation to Generation,* "If one family member can successfully increase his or her threshold for another's pain, the other's own threshold will also increase, thus expanding his or her range of functioning."[3]

One common response is to overfunction. When we have difficulty seeing another person's pain, we often rush in to help them avoid it. This is not always bad—but often it is. Your first question should be, "Is this a situation when I can encourage another to rise to the challenge?" The best thing we could do for our grandson when he was going through separation anxiety was to support him as he dealt with it. It really only lasted a few weeks, but it was hard for us. We had to deal with our own pain, so that he could deal with his. When you choose to encourage strength in others, rather than comforting weakness, you are helping both them and you.

Another way we deal with the pain of others is to underfunction. When they lash out in anger or despair, we accommodate their dysfunction, instead of standing up for ourselves. This is called adaptive behavior. It not only avoids challenging the other to deal with their own pain, but it can also result in us feeling resentful. The self-differentiated person would respond by saying, "I know you are hurting, but I am not your problem. I will walk with you as you try to deal with it, but this is your challenge." I will often offer to pray for them, as well. The important point here is to not cave in to the unreasonable demands of one who is avoiding her own pain while, at the same time, not abandoning her emotionally.

Remember: Focus on encouraging strength in others, not comforting their weakness. The more you deal with your own pain directly and healthily, the better you will be able to do this.

There is a link between pain and responsibility. We can't make another person responsible. In fact, when we try to make someone else responsible, it actually will make them less responsible. Why? Because trying to make them responsible requires us to overfunction because we are unable to deal with our own pain of seeing the other's irresponsibility. Trying to make someone else responsible takes away their responsibility.

The only thing we can do is increase our threshold for their pain. This enables us to allow them to experience the consequences of their own actions. This is hard to do, but it is one of the greatest gifts we can give to another.

When I was upset with my children for not making the bus in high school, I had to learn to deal with my own pain. I was worried about them missing school and thus affecting their academic performance. This was my fear, my pain. By allowing them to miss the bus and then taking them to school on time, I took away any consequences for their actions (or, in this case, inaction). It was only when I informed them, as a non-anxious presence, that if they missed the bus, I would take them to school when I went into the office at 9:00 am, that things began to change. This meant they would miss first period. Once they missed the bus a few times, they figured out how to get up on time on their own.

Loss and Replacement

One of the ways we avoid pain is through replacement. To the extent that we avoid dealing with our grief by replacing the loss, we lose the opportunity to grow.

My mentor who was widowed suddenly was from a generation in which many wives handled all the domestic duties. I have seen numerous instances of men from his generation who were widowed and remarried within a year (some within six months). This is classic pain avoidance through replacement. It's impossible to grieve a loss when you transition that quickly to a replacement for that loss.

My mentor handled it differently. Not only did he lean into his pain, through journaling, but he also focused on becoming self-sufficient. He made a commitment to spend the first year after his wife's death learning to cook, clean, and do laundry. He was determined that he would not even consider another relationship until he had achieved these goals. It may seem that these things have nothing to do with the grief process. In reality, they reminded him of what he had lost and at the same time helped him to envision new possibilities. He ultimately did get remarried, but it was several years later, after he had grieved properly. He even wrote a book on the grief process.

Friedman puts it this way: "To the extent a family rushes to replace loss, its pain will be lessened, but so will the potential for change that the loss made possible".[4] He contends further that replacement is a function of the "residue," that is, the unresolved issues from the lost relationship.

I have officiated a lot of funerals. There are clues to the amount of residue left behind by the deceased. One clue is when there is heightened emotionality. That is, if there is a lot of wailing and moaning before, during, and after the funeral service. The intense emotions might also manifest through conflict among family members. Another clue is when there is a lack of emotion. Everything is stuffed inside, and nothing comes to the surface. Either of these extremes is an indication of unresolved issues with the deceased that continue past his or her death. This is residue.

All families are dysfunctional. Nobody gets the problem

they can handle. But to the extent there was a reasonably healthy relationship, you will find a range of emotions as the family grieves. There will be crying, of course; they are sad. But there will also be laughter. A story will be told, or a family joke is shared, and everybody laughs. There may be some tension, but the importance of honoring the deceased is more important than the differences expressed. This is how the grieving process starts. But it's just the beginning.

The existence of unresolved issues does not guarantee that a replacement will be sought quickly. But it increases the likelihood, because if a person had difficulty with someone when they were alive, they are not likely to suddenly get better at the relationship when they are gone. That being said, it is possible to grieve, to work through the pain, and to get to a new and better place. Even after someone is gone, working through one's own pain and the unresolved issues doesn't require the other to be present. The effect of working through loss is on the one who is grieving. That's why it is a growth opportunity.

It's important to remind you that all change is loss. It's not just death. When a child leaves home to go to college or get a job, this is a loss. How does a parent handle the loss? How does the child? By definition, moving from one job to another is a replacement. So how does one grieve properly?

My own denomination is instructive. We use an "appointment" system to assign clergy to churches. They are "appointed" to serve a church for one year at a time. They could end up serving in a church for a long time, but their appointment is reconsidered each year. The appointment year runs from July 1 of one year to June 30 of the next. Clergy typically find out if they will be reassigned in late winter or early spring, giving them a few months to prepare for their departure. The church will usually find out the name of the replacement within a few weeks to a month after they learn that the current pastor is leaving.

Here is the problem. The denomination has traditionally shunned any sort of transition where the new pastor comes in and spends time with the leadership of the church prior to the transition. So, by definition, there is a quick replacement. Old pastor out on June 30. New pastor in on July 1. But all is not lost. To the extent that the outgoing pastor can help the congregation grieve the loss in advance of her leaving, she can help them make the transition healthier. By connecting emotionally with those with whom she is closest and sharing stories of their time together, she can help the congregation move on. By talking about the transition openly from the pulpit and in leadership meetings, she can help avoid any possible denial of the pending loss. It's not ideal, but it's better than ignoring the situation.

All change is loss. But it is also a growth opportunity. Do you embrace it, deny it, or something in between? Simply understanding the need to deal with loss opens up possibilities. I hope you will take them.

Questions for Reflection:

What change was a large loss for you? How did you handle it?

What is your threshold for the pain of others? How might you increase it?

How can you be more intentional about how you deal with change and loss?

Chapter 4

Triangles

*"You can change yourself and you can change the
situation but you absolutely cannot change other people.
Only they can do that."*

Joanna Trollope

A triangle occurs when two people become uncomfortable in their relationship and they focus on another
person or issue to stabilize it. For example, when two
spouses are uncomfortable in their relationship, they might
focus on the work of one of the spouses as the third side of
the triangle. One spouse may work long hours, while the
other spouse complains about it. By focusing on the work,
they avoid having to deal with their own relationship. This
also highlights the example that a triangle does not have to
include three people. It can be any combination of persons
and issues.

If all change is loss, and somebody finds a replacement for that loss before they have a chance to grieve,

that is a triangle between the person, what is lost, and the replacement.

The Most Stable Form of Relationship

Murray Bowen, the pioneer of family systems theory, believed the triangle to be the most stable form of human relationship. This is because a two-person relationship is inherently unstable. Why? Because the best we can hope for is to be self-differentiated 70 percent of the time. And most of us function that way less than 50 percent of the time. When people are not functioning in self-differentiated ways, they are less willing to take responsibility for themselves. They are unable to tolerate tension in their relationship before resorting to triangling a third person or issue for stability. This ultimately leads to triangles.

There is a paradox in triangles. They are more stable than a two-person relationship, but they create an odd person out. People don't like being excluded. The anxiety generated by this kind of exclusion makes triangles both explosive and difficult to break. In the example given, the odd person out is the spouse who feels excluded by the other's investment in her work. This creates tension and can ultimately lead to conflict. It can also lead to emotional withdrawal. Each of these is a response to being excluded via emotional triangle.

If a triangle is used to stabilize an uncomfortable relationship, there are several ways this can occur.

One is when a person feels like they need more

attention or approval from the other and reacts automatically in immature ways. In this example, the spouse who feels excluded erupts in anger every time the other comes home late from work. Instead of self-differentiating and saying how he would like to spend more time with his wife, he focuses on his wife's job.

Another is when someone has unrealistic expectations of herself or another. In our example, the wife might be using her work to bolster her own self-image. Instead of being comfortable in her own skin, that is, being self-differentiated, she uses the external motivation of succeeding in her work to justify herself. Conversely, she might have unrealistic expectations of her husband, but can't express herself, so she buries herself in her work. People are a mess, and we use endless ways to avoid dealing with our own issues. Nobody gets the problem they can handle.

Another is difficulty in maintaining appropriate boundaries. When one is feeling stress or tension, she might distance herself from the other or become overly intrusive with the other. In our example, the wife could have initially used her job to distance from her husband. Or the husband might have allowed his own anxiety to spill into their relationship the first time she came home late from work. Either of these could have occurred first. Both could be occurring to maintain the triangle. She comes home late. He reacts. She distances herself even more to avoid dealing with him. Did I mention that people are a mess?

Either of these responses is subconsciously intended to relieve anxiety, but instead they increase the discomfort in the relationship, which can result in forming, then maintaining, a triangle.

Here are some other examples of triangles.

One example is two spouses and a child. To avoid self-differentiating with each other, one of the parents, typically the mother, fulfills the unmet emotional needs from her spouse by investing in her child. This leaves the husband on the outside, who usually will be supportive of the over-involvement. In this case, the mother's overfunctioning with the child is complemented by the father's underfunctioning.

Another form of a parent-child triangle occurs when both parents focus all their efforts on developing a skill or talent in a child. This could be dance, music, sports, or academics. Fill in the blank. It's process, not content, which I'll unpack in the next chapter. It is their focus on their child that stabilizes their relationship with each other.

A second example is a parent and two children. The parent is not comfortable with self-differentiating with either of the children, so she calls one whenever she has a problem with the other. "Tell your brother that I don't like how he is handling the family business." Or, "Did you know your sister is letting her son do whatever he wants?" Or, "I'm really angry that your brother is choosing to go to his wife's house for Christmas instead of being with us." You get the picture.

Again, the content can be anything. It's process, not content. And the process is the inability to deal with one's own anxiety in a self-differentiated way, resulting in an emotional triangle.

You Can't Change the Relationship of Others

A guiding principle of emotional triangles is that you can't a change a relationship to which you don't belong. You probably have learned by now that you can't change other people. This applies to triangles. In the first example where the husband is complaining about the amount of time his wife spends working, the complaints will likely not change the situation. In fact, the more time he spends trying to convince her to work less, the more likely it will be that she doesn't.

This is an example of another principle of emotional triangles. When you try to change the relationship of the other two sides of a triangle, it not only strengthens the triangle, but you also will end up with the stress of the situation. The husband will be the one who is feeling left out. The wife will be fine because she has her work to distract her. Paradoxically, if he got out of the triangle in between his wife and her work, he might have a chance. We'll cover that in more depth in the next chapter.

So, it won't be the wife who works too much that feels the stress. It will be the husband who complains. This will likely result in a workaholic wife and a husband who dysfunctions in some other way.

Which leads to the final principle of triangles, which is that triangles interlock. When the complaining spouse gets tired of complaining about his wife's work, he will find something else to do to stabilize that relationship. Perhaps he will focus on complaining about his pastor. Or maybe he will turn to drinking. The least likely thing he will do is to take responsibility for himself.

This final point is our first clue in understanding how to deal with triangles.

Dealing with Triangles

The best way to avoid a triangle is to take responsibility for yourself and nobody else. This is the essence of self-differentiation. But remember, self-differentiation includes both self-definition, which is taking responsibility for oneself, and emotional connection, which is the presence part of being a non-anxious presence.

When someone is triangling you, a helpful way to look at it is to think, "She is uncomfortable with this other relationship, so she is triangling me." By doing this, you can avoid taking it personally and avoid trying to fix the situation. Either action would draw you into the triangle.

The second thing you can do is give her back responsibility for her problem. Instead of taking on her anxiety, you can give it back.

Let's say that a coworker comes to you and complains about another coworker. Alarms should be going off in your head. She is defining your coworker, not defining herself. She is not acting in self-differentiated ways. She is not comfortable with her relationship with your coworker, so she is coming to you.

Here are some things you could say to give the problem back to her.

"Sounds like you really have a problem."

"You're really struggling with this."

"Have you told her how you feel?"

The best thing you can do is not argue, and not agree. If you argue with her, you are basically trying to convince her that she's wrong about the other. If you agree with her, you've been brought into the triangle as an accomplice. I'll go into this further in chapter 7.

I recently had a colleague text me to say he had received a snarky email from someone he served with on a committee. He wrote, "I realized that she was defining me, not herself." What he understood was that when someone is defining you, she is avoiding something in herself. Recognizing this process is essential to avoiding triangles and responding to them in a healthy way. That's the focus of the next chapter.

Questions for Reflection:

How do you handle an uncomfortable relationship? Are you able to take responsibility for yourself, or do you triangle someone or something else?

How are others triangling you?

What can you do to stay connected to those who triangle you, without trying to change them?

Chapter 5

Process Not Content

"We fight a lot, you know, but that's family. We may be dysfunctional but we're still family."

Star Jones

Separating emotional process from content is simple, but it's not easy. It's simple because in any interaction you can ask yourself, "What is the emotional process that is going on?" The content is whatever you're discussing.

It's not easy because most of us are more likely to speak without thinking. We automatically react to whatever is happening. This often takes the form of reactivity, which I'll discuss in greater detail in chapter 6.

Without self-awareness and intentionality, we do life the way we always have. We are on autopilot. This means that we play all the scripts that have been programmed by our family of origin. Whether it's unleashing or stuffing our own anxiety, or reacting to the anxiety of others, our tried and true patterns persist.

The problem is that "tried and true" is more like "tried and failed." Because we typically function in self-differentiated ways about half the time, that means half the time our scripts are not working. We are triangling or being triangled. We are arguing with others or giving in without taking an emotional stand. We are the source of anxiety—or the object of it.

Understanding emotional process gives us a tool to get some perspective. Because it is not related to the content of the matter, it enables us to see things differently. When we view things from the standpoint of process, we are able to better regulate our own anxiety, as well as better able to respond in healthy ways. This starts by understanding the four patterns of interaction.

Four Patterns of Interaction

In any system, there is stress and tension. This is a part of life. The question is: How does the system respond? Family systems theory documents four patterns in the nuclear family.

The first is marital conflict. As stress increases, so does the anxiety of each spouse. Instead of dealing with it in a self-differentiated way, they create triangles. The content could be anything. The other spouse works too much, doesn't pick up their underwear, watches too much TV, spends too much time on social media, doesn't eat enough, ad infinitum. This is triangling: Instead of dealing with whatever stress there is (e.g., money, work, or kids), they focus on something that is wrong with their spouse.

In marital conflict, the other spouse will respond in kind, picking something about the spouse that needs "fixing." This creates a dance where each criticizes the other, each resists being controlled, and the anxiety in the system increases.

The second pattern is when one spouse dysfunctions. This occurs when spouse A reacts to stress as outlined above, by triangling spouse B through criticism and efforts to control. In this case, spouse B adapts by giving in. Instead of standing up for herself, she goes along with spouse A to try to preserve harmony in their relationship. However, she can only do this for so long before her anxiety will increase and, if intense enough, may cause dysfunction in some other way. The symptoms will vary, manifesting in over-eating, high blood pressure, substance abuse, etc. Note that this form of adapting can result in a dysfunction that affects the emotional or physical health of the spouse who is unable to self-differentiate when pressured by the other.

The third pattern is an unhealthy focus on one or more of the children. Instead of triangling each other, they triangle the kids. Typically, one of the parents will focus on one of the kids with either an idealized or a negative view of her ("She's so smart, beautiful, dumb, irresponsible, etc."). This is process, not content.

This intense child-focus results in the child becoming more reactive to the parents, making it less possible for her to self-differentiate. This can result in rebellion or an intense desire to please resulting in adapting. Neither is healthy, often affecting her academic performance, social relationships, or physical or emotional health.

The fourth pattern is distancing emotionally. When the anxiety of the system gets too intense for a poorly differentiated person, one way she will respond is to withdraw emotionally. Instead of reacting or adapting, she pulls away. The extreme case is emotional cut-off where there is no connection with one or more members of the system. If there is any connection in a cut-off relationship it is through triangled third parties. "Tell father I'll speak to him again when he apologizes."

Too much emotional distance creates anxiety in the system. Those who are distancing themselves will be pursued by those who are most anxious. This causes them to want to withdraw even more. This is the problem with the fourth pattern. The problem with the first three patterns is too little emotional distance, which creates conflict or adaptation.

All these patterns represent what is called an anxiety-driven regression. Instead of self-differentiating, people seek to relieve the anxiety of the moment by fighting, triangling, or adapting. From a process standpoint, the key question is whether someone is taking a clearly defined, non-anxious position. If they are, then this is not a regression; this is self-differentiation. If they're not, then they are seeking to relieve their own anxiety in a way that is not healthy for themselves or the system.

The goal of a self-differentiated person in any system is to take responsibility for oneself and no one else, while remaining connected to others in the system, especially the most anxious. Recognizing anxiety-driven regression is the first step. The second is to remain self-differentiated without engaging in content. It's process, not content. This requires understanding emotional space.

Emotional Space

A key concept in emotional process is emotional space. This is not physical space. In fact, a family member will sometimes move far away to unsuccessfully create emotional space. Healthy emotional space is created when people are self-differentiating. If people in the system are able to take non-anxious, emotional stands, then they create breathing room for everyone. In other words, when people can say what they believe while giving others the freedom to disagree, the whole system relaxes. When they don't, the opposite occurs, and anxiety becomes rampant.

The irony is that anxiety is created when there is either too little or too much emotional space.

Emotional space disappears when someone anxiously overfunctions in the emotional space of another. This is typically a parent or a boss but can be any member of the system who is more concerned about defining the other than herself. This often comes in the form of caring too much. As we saw detailed in chapter 2, because she has a low threshold for the pain of the other, she will overfunction, which increases everyone's anxiety.

Conversely, system anxiety will also increase when there

is too much emotional space. This is the fourth pattern of interaction, where someone pulls away emotionally, even to the point of cutting others off. As mentioned above, the least differentiated in the system will anxiously pursue the one who is distancing to try to reconnect. This will make it even more likely that the person who is distancing will pull away.

There is a sweet spot to healthy emotional space. If people are too close, there is no self-definition, which increases anxiety. If there is too much space, there is no emotional connection, with the same result. Healthy emotional space occurs when people define themselves and not others, while staying connected emotionally. The positive impact on healthy emotional space will ripple throughout the system, whether family, congregation, or organization. As long as a few people can maintain their self-differentiation, even through the inevitable sabotage (more on this in chapter 7), it will be more likely that others will become less anxious in the long run.

Identifying Emotional Process

The key to understanding emotional process is recognizing when it is helpful to engage in the content of a situation. The first clue is the level of anxiety. If there is a lot of tension and if anxiety is being unleashed, it's possible that that there is an emotional process issue in play. This is not always the case. Tension can occur even when people are self-differentiating. But tension combined with externalized anxiety is often a sign that content should be avoided.

Another clue is whether people are defining self or others. When they are defining self, especially in a non-anxious way, this is self-differentiation. When they are defining others, especially you, this is not.

One way people do this is through blaming. Rather than taking responsibility for their own condition, they blame other people or forces. Anxious blaming is a sure sign that content should be avoided. If they are blaming you, then you definitely want to avoid content. They are triangling you by making you the cause of their problem. The more you try to defend yourself and argue your case, the less likely they will be to take responsibility for their own situation.

Another form of triangling occurs when they are blaming someone else and asking you to do something about it. This is still avoiding responsibility, but, in this case, you're not the problem. However, the other wants you to be the solution. Again, getting involved will only make it harder for the other to take responsibility for self.

My first Christmas Eve at a new pastorate involved doing "reader's theater" for the candlelight service. Instead of having readers in the pulpit reading Scripture, we had four persons dressed in black, sitting on barstools, reading a dramatized version of the Christmas story from scripts on music stands. This was over two decades ago and, at the time, was pretty radical for a traditional congregation. When I arrived at the church, I was accosted by a woman who was livid about the change. She was in my face claiming this was not her idea of a Christmas Eve service, was an awful idea, and would ruin everybody's evening.

Let's break down the process and the content. There were two process clues. The first was heightened emotionality. Her anxiety was unleashed on me in a verbal barrage. The second clue was blame. She blamed the change in the service on me and focused more on defining me than defining herself. All change is loss, and she wasn't handling it very well. The content, of course, was the Christmas Eve service.

By recognizing the process, I knew that it would be a trap to try to defend the change to the service by trying to convince her that it was a way to reach people who didn't attend church regularly. Arguing content with someone who is not taking responsibility for self will give them the argument they're looking for and will only enable them to continue this avoidance. Getting into content with my congregant in this situation would have enabled her to continue to be angry at the service and at me.

I did my best to respond in my most non-anxious presence. Remember: This doesn't mean you won't feel anxious inside. Most times you will. My anxiety level was through the roof in this situation. But I was able to self-regulate (see more on this in chapter 8) and respond with, "I can always count on you to tell me how you feel." Sometimes God gives me just the right thing to say, and this was one of them. The woman responded with a "Harrumph!" and walked away.

Note the elements of the response. There was no arguing, no agreement, and my response fostered continued connection between us, despite her anger.

When I asked another member of the congregation if this woman was all right, I learned that her daughter had died around Christmas two years prior. Bingo! There was deep pain around Christmas for this woman. That's hard to deal with, making it easy to create a triangle between her grief and the Christmas Eve service (and me). I visited the woman the following week to connect with her and ask her about her daughter. The Christmas Eve service never came up. See? Process, not content.

The important thing about understanding that it's process, not content, is to realize that emotionality needs emotionality to persist. If you get defensive or argumentative, this will maintain the level of anxiety and enable it to continue. Likewise, if you adapt and give in without self-differentiating, it will reduce the anxiety for the moment, but it will allow the other to avoid taking responsibility, and the pattern will repeat. She'll unload, you give in, and everyone's happy (well, you're not).

Learning to identify emotional process is like learning a new craft. At first things will be hard to identify. But, over time, you will get better at noticing anxiety, blame, pain displacement, and the lack of taking responsibility for self. Engaging with others when they are self-differentiating, even if they don't agree, will provide healthy conversation. Avoiding content when people are not, will give them back the responsibility for their own condition. Either way is great.

Questions for Reflection:

What interaction patterns do you recognize in your family of origin?

What emotional processes are involved in these patterns? What is the content?

Is your tendency to get too close or too distant emotionally? Where does that come from?

Chapter 6

The Leverage of the Dependent

*"The willingness to accept responsibility for one's own
life is the source from which self-respect springs."*
Joan Didion

There is a tension in families between individuality and
togetherness. If everybody is acting as an individual,
without emotional connection, it is typically because
the anxiety in the system became so intense that they
couldn't function in connection. If everybody succumbs
to surrounding togetherness pressure, and there is no
individuality, then they have constant connection without
differentiation. This also increases anxiety in the system,
but instead of withdrawing emotionally, people press
even harder to connect. In the first case, there is too much
emotional distance; in the second, there's not enough.

At the one extreme is a family that has very little
connection. They don't call each other, don't get together,
even for special occasions, and may not have seen each

other for years. It's likely this pattern developed because of an inability to function in healthy ways. Anxiety prevailed, and the only way people could deal with it was to completely disconnect. It's easier to never connect than to have to deal with a fight in every conversation. Or, conversely, to feel like you cave in every time because you have no capacity to stand up for yourself in a healthy way.

At the other extreme is the family that is so close that it's suffocating. Everyone must agree, or nothing happens. Often this is driven by a matriarch or patriarch. What they say goes. Everyone falls in line, and the ability to self-differentiate is non-existent. If you do take a non-anxious, emotional stand, the anxiety unleashed on you will whip you back into shape. There is plenty of connection, but no self-definition.

Of course, the balance is a system where people can say what they believe, while giving others the freedom to disagree. This requires at least one person to act in self-differentiated ways. If you're that person, you'll need to be prepared for the anxiety this kind of behavior will provoke. You must be able to maintain a non-anxious presence, even in the midst of emotional sabotage.

In the cut-off system, this will occur when you try to reconnect. Anxious others will perceive it as you trying to tell them what to do. Staying connected without reacting anxiously will be hard. It will feel counterintuitive. But it will give you a chance to get to a new place of both self-definition and emotional connection.

In the suffocating system, self-differentiating will be

about taking a stand; zigging when everyone else wants to zag. This will create havoc. Anxious others will wonder what's wrong with you. But remaining self-defined and non-anxiously connected can start to change the system.

Since every family is dysfunctional to one degree or another, understanding this tension between self-definition and emotional connection is important. To do this, it's helpful to understand the conflict of wills.

The Conflict of Wills

The conflict of wills occurs in a system in which people try to convert others to their own way of thinking. If I am able to say what I believe, then I am self-defining. If I require you to believe the same thing, I am defining you. I'm trying to convince you that I am right, and you are wrong if you disagree with me. This creates surrounding togetherness pressure, which increases anxiety.

The hardest thing to do is to say what you believe while giving others the freedom to disagree. If you can do this, it will reduce the conflict of wills in the system, which will reduce the anxiety. It gives people permission to be themselves, even if that is not what you want them to be. The interesting thing about this is that the more you try to make somebody else in your own image or in an image you want, the more likely they will be to push back and go in the opposite direction. Edwin Friedman has said the hardest thing to do is to push somebody you care about in the direction you fear most.

The conflict of wills can occur in a system where everybody must agree. This is the epitome of surrounding togetherness pressure. A conflict can also occur in a system where people become polarized because certain personalities create division and people have to choose whose side they are on.

This not only increases anxiety, but it also keeps the system stuck as people continue to define others and to try to get them to see their way of thinking, and people push back against that.

The conflict of wills is especially present when a system contains emotionally dependent people.

The Leverage of the Dependent

An emotionally dependent person is one who is unable to define herself apart from another. The typical case might be someone who needs the approval of another to feel validated. The approval might come from a parent, spouse, friend, coworker, boss, or any (or all) of the above. We all like to feel valued, but dependency leaves one feeling anxious and insecure without it.

An article by Leon F. Seltzer, Ph.D. in *Psychology Today* distinguishes between dependency and support. The latter is about healthy emotional connection. Support is having people who care about you and are willing to walk alongside you. Dependency not only requires connection, it requires continual unconditional love, because when we are dependent, we can't validate ourselves. And because dependency is rooted within us, we can never receive enough validation. The more we rely on the reassurance of others, the less capable we will be to value ourselves. Dependency is the opposite of self-differentiation.

Seltzer puts it this way: "The problem here is that it's difficult to love someone—and let them be free to be who they are—when, unconsciously, we need them to help us cover up past insecurities. These insecurities originate much less from our present-day partner as from our earlier history, most often because, while growing up, our parents weren't able to make us feel securely attached to them."

Seltzer doesn't blame the parents (as he shouldn't). He points out that a child is unable to communicate her own emotional needs, that many parents (or caretakers) have little idea of what's really in the best interests of the child, and a parent is not capable of giving a child what they never received in their own upbringing.

This last point is key. This is the family systems concept of generational transmission: We basically pass on what we know, whether healthy or dysfunctional. If you were never loved unconditionally by your parents, it's likely they never felt that either. This doesn't mean you have to withhold that from your own family. It just means that it will be harder to do it naturally. And the best way to do this is to work on yourself first. Learn to value who you are. This will help you to self-differentiate.

At this point, it is helpful to clarify the difference between being dependent, codependent, and interdependent. We have already defined being dependent.

Codependency is a form of dependency with a rather perverse twist. The form of validation required by a codependent person is the need to be needed. They feel worthless unless they are needed to make sacrifices on behalf of another. This need to be needed by the other gives them a sense of purpose.

Of course, it takes two to tango. In a true codependent relationship, the one who is needed is dependent. Either she needs the codependent one to constantly care for her needs, or she is codependent herself. Yes, a codependent relationship can have two people who constantly sacrifice for the other without ever defining themselves. They define themselves by their willingness to care for the needs of the other.

If the partner of a codependent is simply dependent, she comes to rely on the codependent one for validation.

Contrast dependency and codependency with interdependency. Self-differentiated people express themselves in interdependent ways. The heart of this is a healthy emotional connection that values the other without trying to define her. It also values self without needing another to validate or define oneself. Each person is able to express her own emotions and needs, without tugging on the other to meet them. Each one has her own identity that is not defined by the relationship. Let's look at an example.

If a family member (take your pick: spouse, parent, sibling, child) says, "You don't love me if you don't do this for me," then they are acting dependently. The "this" could be anything. Remember: Family systems is about emotional process, not the content of the process.

If you adapt to this demand, that is, give in without an argument, you will perpetuate their dependency. The more you do it, the more they will hold you hostage, and the more resentment you're likely to feel.

If you get personal validation out of doing this, that is, if you willingly sacrifice to meet the demand of the other, then you are codependent. If you say, "I'm sorry I can't do that for you, but I'll try to show you other ways that I love you," Then you're self-differentiating.

In any system, the dependent people have the leverage, but only as long as we let them. They make demands of others, rather than self-differentiating. They need others to feel loved and validated. This holds us hostage, unless we are willing to self-differentiate.

The problem is that if you self-differentiate with the dependent, they will take it personally. The response may vary from anger at you, feeling victimized by you, trying to guilt you into compliance, or some combination of these. It's all about getting you to do what they need so they can feel loved and validated.

This is called sabotage. When you self-differentiate with a dependent person, their anxiety levels will go up, and they will work hard to get you to comply with their demands.

I should note that sabotage is unwitting. I had someone in an online class remark that they did not like the term "sabotage," as it implied intentionality. I get this. But in family systems theory, the idea of sabotage is that the dependent in a system feel uncomfortable with change, so they unwittingly work to change things back.

When someone who is dependent is suddenly faced with a self-differentiating person who no longer complies with her demands, she will get angry, coerce, beg, blame, guilt, plead, or use any other means to get her way. The means themselves will vary, but the process is the same: to put on the full court press to get her way.

If you remain a non-anxious presence in the face of sabotage, the anxiety and pushback will increase. What you are doing is making the dependent one responsible for her own condition. Instead of validating her, you are leaving her to validate herself, without leaving her on her own. That's what it means to be a non-anxious presence. You're not allowing her anxiety to get you to comply with her demands, but you are staying connected to her emotionally.

This is important. If you don't comply, but are not connected, she will continue her dependent ways and will ultimately find other ways to meet her demands. This might be good for you, but it doesn't help her.

We'll dig into how to deal with sabotage in the next chapter. For now, understand that you are not growing unless you experience sabotage. Every system has emotionally dependent people. Change will make them feel uncomfortable. If you are not experiencing sabotage, you are not changing how you function.

Systems get stuck because dependent people make demands and we, when we are unable to self-differentiate, comply with their demands. We think it's easier to give in then to take a stand. Or we take a stand, but we don't connect emotionally. Either case will make things worse.

In the former, the dependent one will continue to make demands, and it will get harder and harder to change. In the latter, where we self-define, but don't stay connected, she will find ways to triangle to express her displeasure.

As long as you focus on trying to change the dependent, you will feel frustration and stress. This is a conflict of wills. For example, if someone makes a demand and says she doesn't feel valued, you try to convince her that you do value her. But no matter what you say, the only way to pacify her is to meet her demand. You're stuck. This is because you're trying to convince her that you do value her, but she doesn't value herself.

Here's the good news. If you focus on self-differentiating, on remaining a non-anxious presence, then you have the leverage. Why? Because now, instead of you having to change her mind, she has to change *your* mind. Instead of you having to convince her that she's valued, she has to convince you to meet her demands. Now she will feel the stress and frustration. That's when the sabotage comes.

If you can maintain a non-anxious presence through the sabotage, you give her a chance to find a new, healthier place of functioning. I've seen this at work in families, congregations, and work systems. It's not easy, but it's the only way.

Questions for Reflection:

What demands do the dependent make on you?

When do you act dependently?

In either of the above situations, what can you do to take responsibility for yourself?

Chapter 7

Sabotage

"The way I see it, it's impossible to change things without encountering resistance."

Evo Morales

Sabotage is a family systems term for the unwitting resistance that occurs in response to change in a family of origin, congregation or work system. Because all change is loss, people must be able to process change in the same way we might grieve the loss of a loved one. Some changes will not be that intense, but the phenomenon is similar.

The problem is that people often don't recognize the need to process change. Further, the less differentiated persons in the system will displace their pain in ways that refuse to take responsibility for themselves. The more people in a system who are less self-differentiated, the greater the overall resistance, or sabotage, will be.

As I mentioned in the last chapter, the resistors do not realize they are engaged in sabotage. But from the standpoint of someone who is trying to make positive change happen, it feels intentional. If you are trying to improve your own functioning, then sabotage is inevitable. As you start to take healthy, non-anxious emotional stands, this will cause upset in the system, and sabotage will occur.

Leading any kind of change is like crossing a busy street. Changing how you function is like getting to the curb; it's the easy part. Dealing with the sabotage that will certainly occur is like getting across the street without getting run over. You must be aware of what's coming at you, or you won't make it.

It's also important to point out that sabotage is inevitable because we humans tend to function lower on the scale of self-differentiation. Remember that the best we can hope for is to function in self-differentiated ways about 70 percent of the time. And most of us are doing this less than 50 percent of the time. This means that when we change, there will be people who are not able to process this in healthy ways. Hence, the sabotage.

Clues You Are Being Sabotaged

There are several clues to recognizing sabotage. The first is the anxiety level of those in the system. If things have changed, how are they functioning? If there is anger, blaming, resentment, or other negative behaviors, it's possible that it's sabotage.

I say possible, because the second clue is recognizing who others are defining. Are they defining themselves or other people? For example, someone may be angry, but she may say it in a healthy way: "I'm angry with you." It's OK to be angry. The question is how is it expressed? Conversely, she could say angrily, "You are making my life miserable!" She is angry, but not taking responsibility for herself. She is defining you, not herself. Pain and blame displacement are classic indications of unresolved anxiety being expressed as sabotage.

The third clue is whether a triangle is involved. As we know, a triangle is a great way to avoid taking responsibility for oneself. If the anxious other complains to you about another in the system, it's possible that this is sabotage—especially if this behavior is new.

For example, let's say that you've started exercising regularly. Suddenly, your father starts complaining to you about your sister-in-law and is on you to talk to your brother about his wife. You say this is unrelated. You say that your father should be happy about you improving yourself. If your father were to ask himself, intellectually, he would say that he is happy for you.

But perhaps this change is causing him discomfort. He's not even aware of it, but he deals with it by triangling you. There's a good chance that, gone unrecognized, this could cause you to feel stressed out, and ultimately might knock you out of your exercise routine. This would be much more likely if you didn't recognize the triangle and felt like you had to talk to your brother. Talk about stress! That's how sabotage works.

Another form of triangle is when someone is triangling

someone else about you. This is classic passive aggressive behavior. They are uncomfortable with the change you are making, so they complain to another. Or they triangle an issue like substance abuse, infidelity, or an obsession with a hobby. In the latter case, a hobby can be a good thing. But if it's a way to avoid taking responsibility for oneself, then it's a triangle.

Regardless of how the sabotage takes place, your main goal is to remain a non-anxious presence. Don't react. Don't adapt. Don't argue, and don't give in. Remain firm in your new functioning, but don't allow others to bait you into a conflict of wills. Their discomfort with your new self is not your problem. It's their problem. Your goal is to not let it be your problem. We'll get into how to do this in the next chapter. For now, remember that lasting change will only occur after you have maintained a self-differentiated presence in the midst of sabotage.

One thing that makes this difficult is empathy.

The Problem with Empathy

In *A Failure of Nerve*, Edwin Friedman maintains that empathy is a problem.[5] He contends that empathy is the source of overfunctioning and enabling behavior; that because of empathy, we are not able to remain self-differentiated in the face of sabotage. I agree to a certain extent, but I think it's a bit more complicated.

To better understand this, I decided to look into empathy.

The current understanding of empathy breaks it down into two types: affective and cognitive. Some say there is a third type, somatic empathy, where "mirror neurons" actually cause us to physically mimic the emotions of another, but the research on this is not conclusive. Anyway, for the purposes of understanding sabotage, distinguishing between affective and cognitive empathy is what matters.

Affective empathy is the ability to respond appropriately to the emotions of others. It is further subdivided into two types of responses: empathic concern and personal distress. Empathic concern is the ability to respond with compassion and care. Personal distress is "self-centered feelings of discomfort and anxiety in response to another's suffering."[6]

I would contend that it is the personal distress response that causes a problem in any system. When people are less differentiated, they are unable to distinguish between the problems of others and their own feelings. In fact, they unwittingly make the problems of others their own problems. This is a problem. Instead of letting the other respond to their own challenges, a personal distress response will result in a need to relieve one's own anxiety. This could be through enabling, overfunctioning behavior. It could also be through blame or pain displacement, either aimed at the other or by triangling a third. Or one could withdraw completely, which is definitely not helpful. I believe it is the personal distress response that Friedman has a problem with.

Conversely, I believe empathic concern is the response of a self-differentiated person. This is appropriate emotional connection. Showing care and concern for another who is in pain is appropriate, as long as you don't try to relieve her pain for her. Remember that affective empathy is the ability to respond appropriately.

The other type of empathy is cognitive empathy. Sometimes called "perspective taking," this is the ability to understand the thinking behind another person's mental state. It's the ability to see things from another's point of view. You don't have to agree with her; you're just able to see things the way she does.

I believe that cognitive empathy is a critical skill in recognizing emotional process. It's not emotional at all. In fact, some would call it cold or calloused. It's getting into someone else's head in a good way, so as to understand where they're coming from. It helps us to recognize whether someone is self-differentiating or not.

When it comes to sabotage, empathy can be a good thing or a bad thing. It's a good thing when you are able to use cognitive empathy to recognize emotional process. This helps keep you from getting sucked in emotionally to the anxiety of others. It enables you to have some perspective on the situation. It provides emotional space to help you avoid reacting. Cognitive empathy can help you recognize sabotage without taking on the problems of others.

Likewise, empathic concern is a good thing. It's how you stay connected emotionally to another without taking on their problems. A healthy combination of cognitive empathy and empathic concern is how you can remain a non-anxious presence in the face of sabotage.

Conversely, personal distress is a form of empathy that will make things worse. It will feed the anxiety of others and make the sabotage harder to handle. Personal distress will cause you to overfunction and/or enable inappropriate behavior. It will result in reactivity, unleashing your own anxiety in the face of sabotage, or adaptivity, which is giving in without taking a non-anxious stand. Neither will get you across that proverbial street.

From a systems perspective, sabotage is inevitable when change occurs. Anticipating it is like looking both ways before you cross the street. It will help you see it coming before it runs you over. Dealing with sabotage is like getting across the street; it requires self-regulation.

Questions for Reflection:

When have you experienced sabotage? What were the clues?

How did you handle it?

How are you most likely to respond to such situations: with empathic concern, personal distress, or cognitive empathy?

Chapter 8

Self-Regulation

"Reactive people . . . are often affected by their physical environment. They find external sources to blame for their behavior."

Stephen Covey

Self-regulation is keeping your anxiety in check so it doesn't make a bad situation worse. That's easier said than done. It takes intentionality and self-awareness. It's important to remember that being self-differentiated doesn't mean you won't feel anxious inside. You will. But you can still be a non-anxious presence if you can self-regulate. To better understand how to do this, it's helpful to understand the family systems concept of reactivity.

Reactivity

By now, you realize that much of your behavior has been inherited from your family of origin. As W. Thomas Soeldner writes:

Where did this automatic emotional reactiveness come from? We learn it in our earliest years in our family of origin and/or with primary caregivers. We are the product of generations of such automatic responses. We receive the family emotionality, i.e. "instincts," from our parents, who received them from theirs, and so on through generations. We learn how to relate to others in interaction with our siblings. It all comes to us without our knowledge or choice-without, that is, until we reach a time of recognition and discernment, and ask ourselves, "Who am I?"[7]

Reactivity is defined as: "The tendency of the organism to respond to perceived threat or the anxiety of others. It is more pronounced at lower levels of self-differentiation."[8]

There are several components here. Let's work backwards.

First is the anxiety of others. This is the easiest to understand, especially when the anxiety is directed toward us as anger or blaming. It's hard to regulate our own anxiety in these situations.

Second is a perceived threat. While the anxiety of others is external, perceived threats are entirely internal. The perceived threat may or may not be real. If what we perceive raises anxiety in us, it is possibly connecting to an unresolved issue in our own family of origin. Why? Because not all threats raise our anxiety. The level to which this will occur is entirely in us. Nobody gets the problem they can handle.

For example, let's say your boss comes to you and says, "You need to get this project finished on time or there's going to be big trouble."

An objective observer might ask, "What kind of trouble?" If you are self-differentiated, you might ask the same question.

But let's say your boss' tone of voice reminds you of your mother, with whom you have been in constant conflict. You feel the anxiety rising in you because you are feeling threatened. Your boss didn't actually threaten you. Perhaps she is worried about her own job and is commiserating with you. The point is, perceived threat is in the eye of the beholder.

The third part of this definition is the response. One response is to unleash our anxiety. This is what most people imagine when they think of reactivity. It's the fight part of the fight or flight mechanism. Sometimes this is literally fighting back. Other times, it's getting defensive. In either case, if this is your response, you are not self-regulating. You are allowing your own anxiety to make a difficult situation worse.

Another form of reactivity is giving in. The family systems term is adaptivity, but it's considered a form of reactivity. That's confusing, because it looks like the opposite of reactivity. The thing to remember is that giving in is still a response. When you give in, you are adapting to the anxiety or perceived threat of the other by stuffing your own feelings and *not* taking a non-anxious, emotional stand. Bill Selby, founder of the Center for Pastoral Effectiveness in the Rockies, has coined the term "adaptive reactivity" to describe this form of response (or lack thereof). This highlights the giving-in nature, while noting that in family systems theory this is still considered a reactive response.

Whether a response is adaptive or reactive, it's still not a healthy way to function. Being adaptive does not allow your feelings to be expressed in a healthy way. Being reactive allows your own anxiety to come out in unhealthy ways.

Let's recap. Reactivity is defined as: "The tendency of the organism to respond to perceived threat or the anxiety of others. It is more pronounced at lower levels of self-differentiation."

There is either anxiety or a perceived threat from the other. We either adapt or react instead of taking a non-anxious, emotional stand.

The kicker is that reactivity will increase at lower levels of self-differentiation. Remember that self-differentiation isn't static. Rather than saying you are self-differentiated, it's more accurate to say you are functioning in self-differentiated ways. When you are functioning at lower levels of self-differentiation, you are more likely to react or adapt to the anxiety or perceived threats from others.

I recently got in a fight with my wife. It doesn't happen very often, but the pattern is familiar. She'll make a remark that strikes me the wrong way. Instead of being intentional and thinking about my response, I'll just react. In this case, I got defensive. This starts a pattern of her saying something, to which I respond with greater anger. This can go on for several hours until one of us erupts, we have it out, and then we eventually come to our senses.

The interesting thing about the recent fight was how we unpacked it that evening. She admitted she had been in a bad mood. But then she said, "You're the self-differentiation guy. You're supposed to recognize that and not react."

The truth hurts.

The point about reactivity is that sometimes we're better able to self-regulate than others. Self-differentiation is fluid and can be influenced by the amount of stress you are facing, as well as whether you are sleep-deprived or hungry. So, by definition, self-regulation is keeping your reactivity in check.

Before we get to how to do this, I want to unpack the nature of chronic conditions.

Chronic Conditions

In family systems theory, a chronic condition is a pattern of reactivity that occurs repeatedly. It can be either ongoing or recurring, but, like my fight with my wife, there is a pattern to it. If you have an ongoing interaction with a family member that is filled with anxiety, then it is likely a chronic condition.

The key point to understand is that a chronic condition is sustained by feedback, and that feedback is reactivity. Without a reactive or adaptive response, a chronic condition will disappear. An illustration will help.

Marshall Goldsmith is a world-renowned business educator and coach. In his book *Triggers,* Goldsmith shares a story about Amy, a fifty-one-year-old senior executive at a media company.

> Amy described a close mother-daughter relationship, perhaps too close. Her mother was in her late seventies and they spoke daily, but the conversation was governed by sniping and petty arguments. Parent and child were each engaged in a zero-sum game of proving herself right and the other wrong. "Love by a thousand cuts," Amy called it. One day, triggered by her mother's mortality and the realization that neither of them was getting younger, Amy decided on a truce. She didn't tell her mother about it. She simply refused to engage in the verbal skirmishing. When her mother made a judgmental remark Amy let it hang in the air like a noxious cloud, waiting for it to vaporize from neglect. With her daughter unwilling to counterpunch, Mom soon stopped punching. And vice versa.[9]

This was a chronic condition. The pattern of interaction was the mother making a comment and the daughter reacting. It was only when the daughter decided to regulate her reactivity that the pattern changed. I love Goldsmith's metaphor of the "noxious cloud." Anxiety is like that. But without reactivity, it will dissipate.

It's important to note that a chronic condition can also be sustained by an adaptive response. Using Amy as an example, let's say she never argued with her mother but just "took it." If she never reacted anxiously, let alone never took a non-anxious emotional stand, than she was responding adaptively. It's likely that Amy would then triangle someone else, taking out her frustration and pain elsewhere because she's unable to stand up to her mother in a healthy way.

Either way, it is the reactive or adaptive response that sustains the chronic pattern of anxious interaction.

So now that you understand reactivity and the nature of chronic conditions, it's time to look at how to self-regulate. The best way to do this is to listen.

Listening Is Your Best Response

Responding to the anxiety or perceived threat of others without reactivity is a challenge. The very nature of the interaction increases your own anxiety. But there is a simple way to self-regulate, and that is by listening.

By definition, listening is maintaining a non-anxious presence. One, you are remaining non-anxious because instead of fighting, getting defensive, or caving in, you are asking questions. Two, because you are exploring the other's feelings, you are emotionally present.

The best way to handle an anxious attack by another is to not argue and to not agree. Listening accomplishes this.

You can follow three steps to self-regulate.

First, take a deep breath. Deep breathing is a proven way to physically reduce your anxiety. It also allows you to take your time. When things get anxious, the anxiety of the situation increases our need to respond immediately, so we either blurt out our argument or we immediately agree.

If you can convince yourself that it's OK to be thoughtful, then you can take your time to respond. You can even say something like, "I need a minute to think about this." This also gives you time to increase your self-awareness and intentionality. This will improve your ability to self-regulate.

Next, ask an open-ended question. These are questions that begin with who, what, where, when, and how. Avoid questions that begin with "why." People don't always know why they feel the way they do, so this might increase their frustration. Here are some examples:

"What makes you feel that way?"

"When does this happen?"

"How does that make you feel?"

The list of questions you could ask is endless. Continue to ask open-ended questions. Over the course of the conversation, the anxiety will start to dissipate.

I would suggest practicing asking open-ended questions in non-anxiety producing situations. Do this during meetings at work or church. Do this in routine conversations with family members. The more you practice, the easier it will be to do this when you're feeling most anxious.

Finally, at appropriate times, reflect back what you sense the other is feeling.

"You're feeling angry."

"I sense you are frustrated."

"You feel hurt."

Even if you misjudge them, they will usually appreciate that you are trying to understand them. Regardless, continue with open-ended questions and reflecting their feelings for as long as you can.

I've found that in most cases the anxiety will dissipate pretty quickly. Without reactivity, the noxious cloud dissipates. It's not uncommon for this to be the end of it. The other will say, "I just needed to vent," will thank me, and will move on.

In cases where the other is demanding a response, your best option is to buy some time. Say, "I'd like to think and pray about this. Let me do that and then I'll get back to you." You will have to get back to them, but this will give you more time to process the interaction, as well as increase your self-awareness and intentionality. It will also give you time to practice taking a non-anxious emotional stand when you do respond.

Even more helpful than self-regulating is the ability to use paradox and playfulness to avoid being triangled, to defuse anxiety, and to give back responsibility for oneself. We'll cover that next.

Questions for Reflection:

Are you more likely to respond to an anxious situation with reactivity or adaptivity? Where does that come from?

What chronic conditions exist in your family of origin?

How can you self-regulate to avoid providing the feedback that sustains these conditions?

Chapter 9

Paradox and Playfulness

*"How wonderful that we have met with a paradox. Now
we have some hope of making progress."*

Niels Bohr

What do you do when somebody tells you to do something you don't want to do? How do you express that you disagree with somebody's opinion when they are passionately expressing it in ways that make you feel anxious?

In family systems theory, standing up for yourself in a healthy way is called taking a non-anxious emotional stand. If self-regulation is the non-anxious part, the other part of it is the emotional stand. This involves speaking up for yourself. It's expressing your feelings. It's saying what you believe.

A non-anxious emotional stand is doing this in a non-reactive way. It is neither fighting back, getting defensive, nor giving in. It's the ability to say what you believe in a healthy way.

My own experience is that this does not come naturally. I've had to work on it for a long time. In many situations, I still find it hard to do. One of the major reasons this is true for me, and for most people, is the problem of seriousness.

The Problem of Seriousness

Seriousness is a funny thing. In life, you have to be serious, or you will be irresponsible. You have to show up to work on time, pay your bills, and take out the garbage. If you don't pay attention, your life will become a mess. Life is hard enough without being irresponsible.

However, if you are too serious, you get anxious. This is the problem.

Nobody gets the problem they can handle. If we could handle it, then it wouldn't be a problem. It's often our super serious efforts to deal with a challenge that makes it a problem.

How can you be responsible without being too serious? One way is to remember that you can only be responsible for yourself. Another is to remember that it's often our serious, anxiety-laden efforts that turn a challenge into a problem and a simple problem into a chronic one.

In the last chapter I discussed the nature of chronic conditions. These are perpetual or recurring patterns of anxiety that result in resistance, conflict, anger, and resentment. It's that ongoing fight that you have with a loved one. It may not happen all the time. It may not even happen often. But when it does happen, you know exactly how it's

78

going to go down. You can predict how it will start, what each person will say, and even how it will end. This is a chronic condition.

As we discussed earlier, a chronic condition requires feedback to remain chronic. Feedback can be either reactive or adaptive. Reactive feedback happens automatically and is laced with anxiety. It can be defensive or argumentative. Adaptive feedback is also automatic but it involves giving in. It's not standing up for yourself, even when you don't agree with what the other person is saying.

When someone attacks you anxiously, don't fight back. Don't argue, but don't agree. This is easier said than done, but as I said, the easiest way to do this is to listen.

Listening also will help you to separate process from content.

Emotional process is the systems aspect of what is going on. Are you being triangled? Is the other displacing pain? Are they defining themselves, someone else, or me? Are they taking responsibility for their own position, or are they blaming others?

It comes down to self-differentiation. If the other person is taking a non-anxious emotional stand, then, process-wise, they are self-differentiating, and you should feel free to engage in the discussion. It will be easier, too, because they aren't unleashing their own anxiety on you.

However, if they are anxiously defining you, then you want to avoid the content of the situation. They could be blaming you or anxiously trying to tell you what to do. Here are two examples.

"I feel that your decision has some significant risks that I'd like for us to consider."

"You are risking everything we've worked for with your irresponsible decision."

There are two emotional process clues: the amount of anxiety and the level of self-definition. The first statement is non-anxious and self-defined. It's a non-anxious emotional stand. The second statement is filled with anxiety and is defining the other.

In the former case, you should feel free to have a discussion, making sure to define yourself in a healthy way. Say what you believe while giving the other person the freedom to disagree.

In the latter case, if you get into the content of the situation by arguing or getting defensive, you will be providing the reactive feedback that will make the situation worse and perhaps chronic. Likewise, if you just give in, you will be encouraging the other to railroad you at will.

Notice that the content of the situation is not mentioned. The content could be anything. It could be what you're doing with the family savings. It could be a business decision. It could be a career move.

The point is that understanding the emotional process in the situation will help you to decide when to engage and when to avoid getting into the content of the situation. In the latter case, don't argue and don't agree. But sometimes listening is not enough. The anxiety of the other is so intense that they won't let you off the hook. They demand a response. They want you to engage. They've come looking for a fight, and they won't quit until they get it.

In these cases, you need to understand paradox and playfulness.

Paradox

I was running one morning when a woman came out into her yard with a German shepherd. The dog immediately barked and moved toward me. She yelled, "Don't worry, he's friendly." I've been running for nearly a decade. I've seen a lot of dogs, so I wasn't worried. However, this one came out of the yard, barking at me the whole time, and followed me at a distance of about twenty feet.

A little background here. My experience with German shepherds is not great. My family had a German shepherd named Fritz when I was very young. I don't actually remember him. The family story is that he bit so many people they had to give him up to be a police dog. He was very good at that.

We also had a German shepherd in our neighborhood named Roddy. We thought he was very fierce. One day my friend and I were racing down the street. My friend strayed ever so slightly into Roddy's yard. It was enough for Roddy to fire out from the house at lightning speed and attack. Roddy bit him in the shoulder, although he didn't break the skin. Still, it was a scary scene.

These thoughts flashed in my mind as this German shepherd followed me. But I also knew that the only way he might stop following me was if I turned around and ran back toward his house. That's what I did. He immediately backpedaled and kept his distance. As I ran toward him, he ran back toward his yard. I ran far enough that his owner could grab him by the collar. She said, "Thank you." I turned around and went on my way. This is how dealing with our own anxieties works. It's counterintuitive. Edwin Friedman said in a lecture that the hardest thing to do is to push your loved ones in the direction you fear most.

We've covered how chronic conditions require feedback to be sustained. Without reactive or adaptive feedback, the anxiety dissipates. In these situations, Friedman suggests that you think of yourself as an electrical transformer.[10] You can increase the level of anxiety in the situation with your own reactivity. Conversely, you can act as a step-down transformer to reduce the anxiety, or perhaps even be a circuit breaker where it dissipates altogether.

Paradox can reduce the anxiety of a situation. Think of a tug-of-war; the tension in the rope is the amount of anxiety in the system. The more reactive you get, the harder you tug, the greater the tension in the rope. When both sides are pulling with all their might, the tension is at its max.

But what if you were to walk toward the other? There would be no tension. If you time it right, the other will fall on her butt.

Paradox is like this. Instead of giving someone the fight they're looking for, we go in the opposite direction. Don't argue, and don't agree. It is doing the opposite of our own instincts.

In a 1994 episode of the TV comedy *Seinfeld*, the hapless

George Constanza realizes that every decision he's ever made has been wrong. His revelation is that if his instincts are wrong, he should do the opposite. This approach helps him strike up a conversation with a pretty woman, gets him a job with the New York Yankees, and enables him to take a stand with some rowdies in a movie theater.

Paradox is not reverse psychology. The effect is to help you avoid being reactive. It's paradoxical. The paradox here is to give the other the freedom to make her own decisions. It's exactly the opposite of what we think we should do. By avoiding reactivity, you give back responsibility for another's own destiny. They may not like it, but they'll have to deal with it.

Our younger daughter, the second of our four children, decided to get married this year in Thailand. She and her husband met there while traveling. Their wedding day was ten years to the day after they met. The wedding was immediate family only. This created some anxiety, because weddings in our extended families have typically been large celebrations where we love to be together.

The surrounding togetherness pressure I felt was to convince our daughter to include aunts, uncles, cousins, and my mother, her only remaining grandparent on my side of the family. In fact, my mother, who is ninety-six, has been on our daughter for years to get married. She would say, "I want to see you two get married before I die. I'm not going to be around much longer." But I also realized that this was our daughter's wedding, and to the extent that I pressured her to conform, I would be creating a problem that didn't need to exist. It's also important to recognize that surrounding togetherness pressure can be more perception than reality. Our family members are nice, reasonable people. They might be disappointed, but that's because they love us.

The moment of truth came when we had a family gathering seven months before the wedding. I was sitting next to my mother, and I decided to break the news. I told her our daughter was getting married in Thailand.

My mother responded, "Thailand! That's really far. I don't know that I want to travel that far for her wedding."

My response was paradoxical. "That's OK," I said, "You're not invited." I went on to tell her it was immediate family only.

She thought a moment, then said, "Oh. OK."

What makes paradox so hard is our own anxiety. It's our super-seriousness. We feel like we need to fix the situation when, in reality, there is nothing we can fix. The other will have to fix herself, and we need to get out of the way. Paradox does that. So does playfulness.

Playfulness

Playfulness is a form of paradox that can bring down the anxiety level in the room. It requires the ability to recognize emotional process, so you can avoid getting into content. It's another way to avoid arguing and agreeing, but it is more active than listening.

The primary effect of playfulness is to free us from the seriousness of the situation. The secondary effect is to do the same for others. Most importantly, it avoids reactivity.

The problem is, it's difficult to be playful with those for whom we feel responsible. This is where self-differentiation comes in. To the extent that we are able to self-differentiate, we will only take responsibility for ourselves and not for others. This makes it easier to be playful.

One Sunday our family gathered for lunch after church. It was a sunny day as we sat on a restaurant deck overlooking a river. It was great to be together. At one point, my wife exclaimed, "We have the best family in the world!" We all agreed. But the moment was fleeting.

A few minutes later our two sons, both adults, started arguing about mortgages. One had worked in the mortgage industry. The other was working in it now. Like most children, our boys fought quite a bit growing up, but as adults they've been reasonably well-behaved. Not this day. One of them finally said, "You're not listening to what I'm saying." There was silence. The anxiety was palpable. I found a way to be playful and said, "We used to have the best family in the world!" We all laughed and moved on.

Despite how it appears, playfulness is not about one-liners and quick comebacks. In fact, if it comes across as sarcastic, it will make the situation worse. It's about keeping your own anxiety in check, as well as avoiding the content of the situation. In the case of our sons, there was nothing any of us could do about their bickering. If I had tried to get them to agree or to patch things up, I would have been ignoring the principle of triangles that says I can't change the relationship of two others. Their relationship is their responsibility, and the best thing I can do is to stay out of it, while loving each of them for who they are. What the playfulness did was help me to remain non-anxious. It helped the others in our group do the same.

It's hard to be paradoxical or playful in the moment. Self-regulating helps, since it gives you a chance to recognize emotional process. It also enables you to think about how you might respond with paradox or playfulness. It won't always work, but at least you have a chance.

Another helpful practice is to reflect on your most anxiety-producing situations, especially the chronic ones, and especially the ones in your family of origin. Recognize the emotional process at work. Think about the patterns of reactivity that occur. Then think about how you can respond differently, paradoxically, playfully. This is where it's helpful to have a coach or therapist who can take you through the emotional process and help you practice your responses.

The thing to remember is this: Reactivity doesn't work. It makes things worse.

So far, I've focused on ways to avoid arguing or agreeing, so you can avoid reactivity. But sometimes you will need to take a non-anxious emotional stand.

How to Take a Stand

I define a non-anxious emotional stand as saying what you believe while giving the other the freedom to disagree.

The first step in standing up for yourself is taking

responsibility for yourself by defining your own position. This is usually best done with an "I" statement. Say what you believe while keeping your own anxiety in check.

The next step is to give the other the freedom to disagree. You can say something like, "This is where I'm coming from. You don't have to agree with me, I just want you to know how I feel." This is really important, because people don't like to be told what to do. They don't like to be told what to believe. They don't want to be told how to think.

While it's possible you will still get into a fight with this approach, you can be guaranteed that you'll get into a fight if you make it a win-lose situation. Trying to convince the other to agree with you creates a conflict of wills. This raises anxiety and increases the likelihood of a reactive response.

Finally, stay connected emotionally. Even if she unloads her anxiety on you, try to remain a non-anxious presence. Communicate that you care for her and that it's OK with you if she doesn't agree. Better yet, find a way to be playful and paradoxical. This will help reduce your own anxiety, as well as that of those in the room.

While what I have shared seems like a technique to manage relationships, it's more a way of being. It's intended to help you manage yourself, not others.

This work takes a lifetime.

Questions for Reflection:

In what situations are you too serious?

How can you use paradox and playfulness to regulate your own anxiety without being reactive?

Where do you need to take a non-anxious emotional stand? How will you go about it?

Chapter 10

Doing Your Own Work

"Now, with God's help, I shall become myself."

Søren Kierkegaard

All I've written so far assumes that you are willing to do your own work. This means working on taking responsibility for yourself—and only yourself. It means learning how to take non-anxious emotional stands with those who make you most anxious. It means learning more about your family of origin, and then learning to function in it in healthier ways.

You bought this book for a reason. You've (presumably) read the first nine chapters. With God's help, you can do it. But *you* have to do it. Nobody else can do it for you (and you should wary of those who try).

If you read *Anxious Church, Anxious People*, this chapter will look familiar. It's nearly identical to the last chapter of that book. But whether you're seeking to grow as a family member or as a leader, the process is the same.

What to Expect

According to Jenny Brown from the Family Systems Institute, there are three stages in working toward self-differentiation.[11]

These are:

Stage 1: Reduce anxiety by learning how symptomatic behavior, either that of yourself or others, is part of relationship patterns in the system. This can be both in the congregational system and in the family of origin. It is working through anxiety in the latter that will enable better functioning in all relationships.

Stage 2: Focus on the ability to self-define to increase self-differentiation, while resisting the pull of surrounding togetherness pressures. You articulate your own goals and values and identify the surrounding togetherness pressures that make it difficult to self-define. You do this in a safe place without actually trying to change how you relate in the system.

Stage 3: Learn how to function in self-differentiated ways. This is a coaching process where you anticipate situations in your family of origin that increase anxiety, and then practice how you can function as a non-anxious presence. This will increase your ability to self-differentiate in all situations, including your nuclear family and the congregational system. It's important to remember that self-differentiation includes both self-definition and emotional connection. During this stage you learn to take emotional stands while staying connected to those who make you the most anxious.

Brown writes, "The goal of therapy is to assist family members towards greater levels of differentiation, where there is less blaming, decreased reactivity and increased responsibility for self in the emotional system."[12] This is done by identifying the relationships in your family of origin that cause you the most anxiety, unearthing what makes them anxiety producing, then reworking how you function in those relationships to better self-differentiate. It is not easy work. It is likely to be painful. The thought of taking emotional stands in your most challenging relationships will scare you. The choice is yours. You can do something about your anxiety, or you can leave things alone.

You've come this far. You might as well get started. So let's look at the tools that you'll use to do your own work.

The Genogram

The genogram is both your foundation and your road map. It gives you a way to organize all your thoughts and to learn about your family of origin. It also points you in the right direction to understand which relationships have unresolved issues.

A genogram is a family tree. It is diagrammed in the same way. Each generation is on its own horizontal level. Older generations are higher, and younger generations are lower. There are also lines or markings to indicate emotional distance such as appropriate closeness, fusion (too close), cut-off (too distant), and conflict. There are shadings to indicate physical or psychological illness. There are markings to represent marital status, as well as childbearing events such as adoption, miscarriage, and abortion.

The point here is not to teach you how to do a genogram. It's to help you understand how this graphic representation can help you understand the emotional patterns in your family of origin. Much of what you discover will seem obvious. But it's likely that you have been ignoring or even denying its existence. This will be especially true if you have trouble managing anxiety.

Your genogram will help you identify where you have unresolved issues in your family of origin. Let's face it. We all have issues. Nobody gets the problem they can handle. This truly is the beginning of doing your own work. Once you identify the source(s) of your anxiety, you can then begin the work of changing how you function. It's hard work, but it's worth it.

The Family Timeline

Like the genogram, the family timeline is another tool that will help you understand your family of origin. The purpose is to lay out the arc of your family history, as well as the significant events that help define your family. You should do a separate timeline for both the maternal and paternal sides of your family. Depending on how long you have been an adult, you may want to do another timeline that starts with you and includes your own significant events, relationships, and offspring, if you have any.

The overall arc includes emigrations, relocations, employment changes, births, deaths, marriages, divorces, military service, etc. You also can provide world or regional events that help provide context. For example, the Japanese invasion of Pearl Harbor in 1941 changed everything for both sides of my family. My mother and siblings were living with their aunt in Japan while her parents ran the family business in Seattle. War between the U.S. and Japan created an uncertainty about whether the family would ever be reunited. I know they ultimately were, but the uncertainty itself can be identified as a source of anxiety in the system. Likewise, my father's family was relocated from their home in Seattle to an internment camp in Idaho. Pearl Harbor was the defining moment that started this process.

Your timeline will be most useful if you include other significant, family-defining events. Examples include: arrests and imprisonments; betrayals; business formations or breakups; prolonged battles with disease; and the origins of ongoing disputes. Your family timeline can include anything that you or another family member recalls quickly as something that has shaped who you are. It will take some time to do, but it is worth the effort, because it will help you to decipher the code that defines your family.

The Importance of Stories

The genogram and family timeline will require you to speak to family members. More importantly, it will require you to listen to their stories. This may be intimidating, but there's no way around it. This is how you will crack the code to your family of origin.

The most daunting part will be engaging with those who make you most anxious. This is especially true if that person is a parent. The best way to approach this is to start somewhere else. If you have living grandparents, they are a great source of stories. Not only will you hear stories that help you understand the family, you will also hear stories about your parents from an entirely different perspective. Aunts and uncles are another great source. It's likely that they and you will feel much lower emotional stakes. Because they aren't your parents, they may share things that they wouldn't with their own children. They can provide perspective on your parents and grandparents that illuminate your understanding of your family's functioning.

Anxiety is transmitted from generation to generation. Most times it's done unknowingly. Molly S. Castelloe, Ph.D. cites the work of M. Gerard Fromm in her *Psychology Today* article, "How Trauma Is Carried Across Generations: Traumatic events can be passed onto the next generation." She writes:

"The transmission of trauma may be particular to a given family suffering a loss, such as the death of an infant, or it can be a shared response to societal trauma. Maurice De Witt, a sidewalk Santa on Fifth Avenue noticed a marked change in behavior the holiday season following 9/11 when parents would not 'let the hands of their children go. The kids sense that. It's like water seeping down, and the kids can feel it... There is an anxiety, but the kids can't make the connections.'

"This astute man was noticing a powerful double message in the parent's action," Fromm says. "Consciously and verbally, the message was 'Here's Santa. Love him.' Unconsciously and physically, it was 'Here's Santa. Fear him.' The unnamed trauma of 9/11 was communicated to the next generation by the squeeze of a hand."

Psychic legacies are often passed on through unconscious cues or affective messages that flow between child and adult. Sometimes anxiety falls from one generation to the next through stories told."[13]

It's hard to overestimate the importance of releasing the anxiety of unresolved issues. Sometimes we don't even know that the anxiety exists.

95

My mother was born in Seattle in 1923. Her father and his brothers owned a wholesale seafood business. They were the first non-Anglo business on the Seattle waterfront. But my grandfather sent the family back to Japan in 1933 to help the business survive the Great Depression. Her mother came back to Seattle a few years later to be with her husband. My mom and her four siblings stayed with their aunt in Hiroshima until 1947.

I grew up hearing my mother's stories of life in Japan. Most of them centered around what life was like being separated from her parents while her own country (the U.S.) and her country of origin and residence (Japan) were at war. Some of her stories were about the A-bomb. Her family was fortunate. Of the five children, only the youngest, Nobu, was killed in the blast. She was fifteen years old. I don't know if the stories transmitted anxiety or not. I do know that I'm glad they were told.

Six years ago my aunt called me on my birthday. She doesn't usually call. When she did, she said, "Happy Birthday! Same birthday as Nobu."

I wanted to say, "What! I have the same birthday as my aunt who was killed by the A-bomb, and nobody told me?" I thanked my aunt for telling me and told her that I had never known this, using the best non-anxious response I could muster. Then I called my mom and asked her about it.

"What? Hmmm. Oh yeah, I guess you do have the same birthday. I guess I forgot about it."

I wonder what anxiety was transmitted by not telling me? I wonder what anxiety was released when I found out?

I can't really answer it, but it felt like a good thing to find out. It binds me in a special way to my family heritage that I can't explain.

As my own experience demonstrates, you won't always understand everything you learn. You won't be able to assign value to all that you hear. Listening to your family's stories is just the beginning. You then need a way to process it.

You Can't Do This Alone

Doing your own work requires you to go deeper into your relationships in order to unpack and decode the unwritten rules of your family system. You can do a lot of thinking about this, but it's impossible without help. Fortunately, you have options.

The best option is to find a family systems therapist. Family systems theory was developed by Murray Bowen, so you want to find someone who specializes in family systems therapy or Bowenian family therapy. This doesn't mean you need to bring your whole family into sessions with your therapist. It means she will help you to view your situation from a systems perspective and will help you work through the stages of the self-differentiation process. If your family of origin is characterized by one or more of the following situations, it may be impossible to do your own work without a professional therapist:

➢ Constant, debilitating anxiety and conflict

→ Emotional cut-offs—meaning people do not speak to each other for months or years at a time due to unresolved conflict

→ Intense trauma such as abuse, violence, or forced separations

Anyone can benefit from seeing a therapist, but the greater the unresolved issues, the more necessary a therapist becomes.

Another option is to find a coach who uses a family systems approach. This is not a professional therapist, but someone who has done their own work and understands how to walk you through the process. Coaching can be done one-on-one or in a group setting. The coach will help you to use the tools already described so you can work your way through the stages of the self-differentiation process. You may want to work with a coach for a limited period of time, perhaps six months to a year. Or, like a therapist, you may feel the coach can help you over the long-term to modify your input into the systems to which you belong, both as a family member and as a leader.

Finally, you can find a program that specifically focuses on the family systems approach to congregational leadership. I list several of these in the resource section of this book. These are comprised of a series of multiday workshops or retreats where you will do your own work, all within the context of serving in the church. You will be with the same cohort of persons throughout the process, which makes the process a combination of group learning and group coaching.

You may find that you use more than one of these approaches. This is a life's work. If the best we can hope for is 70 percent self-differentiation, then there is always room to improve. But the benefits are priceless. You will be a better family member, a better person, and a better leader.

It's Your Move

What happens next is up to you. You can set this book down and get on with your life. Or you can start (or continue) your journey toward greater self-differentiation. You can try to lead change, only to retreat when the sabotage gets too intense. Or you can find yourself and, in the process, discover how you can sustain a non-anxious presence in the midst of anxiety and resistance. If you are willing to make the effort, you can expect to be able to:

- ⇢ Articulate your values, beliefs, and vision, while giving others the freedom to disagree, even in the midst of surrounding togetherness pressures

- ⇢ Better recognize emotional triangles

- ⇢ Work to remain a non-anxious presence in the triangles to which you belong

- ⇢ Better manage stress

→ Better regulate your own anxiety and your input into the systems to which you belong

→ Stop trying to convince others to agree with you, and believe instead in what God is leading you to do

→ Discern the difference between those who are trying to help you and those who are trying to change you

The list goes on. By now you get it. Your willingness to do what is necessary to grow in your self-differentiation can make all the difference in your life and the life of your family. The question is: What will you do next?

It's your move.

Appendix

I t may be time for you to read or reread Edwin Friedman's books. I've mentioned two of the three already.

Generation to Generation: Family Process in Church and Synagogue
The seminal work that applies Murray Bowen's family systems theory to congregational leadership. It is difficult material, but after reading my book, it may be easier to understand. It has been my constant companion throughout my ministry.

Friedman's Fables
Just as Jesus told parables to illustrate concepts of God's reign, Friedman uses fables to help us understand family systems. You could actually use this book without *Generation to Generation*, but it's best to use them together.

A Failure of Nerve: Leadership in the Age of the Quick Fix
Friedman was working on this book when he died in 1996. It was completed by his family and colleagues and

published ten years after his death. It takes Generation to Generation a step further and applies it to the larger society with amazing insight.

Programs to Do Your Own Work

The following programs can help you do your own work without a therapist. This is a personal decision. Many people are able to do this. Some are not. If you try this approach, you can always decide to see a therapist if you realize you need more help.

I've listed programs that can help you work through your own functioning in your family of origin. They are designed for leaders in the congregational context. I know those who lead these programs and/or have heard positive feedback from people who have participated in them. There are certainly others, but I can only recommend those I know.

I've listed the Center for Family Process first, since this was founded by Edwin Friedman.

Center for Family Process
Bethesda, MD
www.centerforfamilyprocess.com

Center for Clergy Excellence
Centreville, MD
www.pecometh.org/clergy-excellence

Center for Pastoral Effectiveness of the Rockies
www.pastoraleffectiveness.org

Lombard Mennonite Peace Center
Lombard, IL
www.lmpeacecenter.org/workshops/lac

Tending the Fire
Northeastern U.S.
www.tending-the-fire.com

About the Author

Jack Shitama is an ordained United Methodist minister and the founding Minister-in-Residence of the Center for Clergy Excellence in Centreville, MD. He loves to help others become their best through his writing, teaching, speaking and coaching. His podcast, *The Non-Anxious Leader Podcast* is available on all platforms.

Jack is an avid runner and has completed the Baltimore Marathon three times. He and his wife, Jodi, have four adult children, one grandchild, and two on the way. They live with no kids and no pets on Maryland's Eastern Shore.

You can subscribe to his blog, as well as find out more about him, at *www.thenonanxiousleader.com*.

You can contact him at *jack@christian-leaders.com*.

Notes

1.   Edwin H. Friedman, *Generation to Generation: Family Process in Church and Synagogue* (New York: The Guildford Press, 1985), 27.

2.   American Psychological Association, https://www.apa.org/ HELPCENTER/road-resilience.

3.   Friedman, 47.

4.   Friedman, 42.

5.   Edwin H. Friedman, *A Failure of Nerve: Leadership in the Age of the Quick Fix* (New York: Seabury Books, 1999, 2007).

6.   Wikipedia.com, "Empathy," https://en.wikipedia.org/wiki/ Empathy.

7.   W. Thomas Soeldner, "Resilience: Nature's Imaginative Response to Challenge," https://systems-coaching.com/ principal-facilitatorcoach/.

8.   Familysytemstheory.org, "Glossary of Terms: Reactivity," http://www.familysystemstheory.org/glossary-of-terms/.

9.   Marshall Goldsmith, Mark Reiter, *Triggers: Creating Behavior That Lasts—Becoming the Person You Want to Be* (New York: Crown Business, 2015), 221.

10. Friedman, *Generation to Generation*, 208-209.

11. Jenny Brown, "Bowen Family Systems Theory and Practice: Illustration and Critique," The Family Systems Institute, http://www.thefsi.com.au/wp-content/uploads/2014/01/Bowen-Family-Systems-Theory-and-Practice_Illustration-and-Critique.pdf, 6.

12. Brown, "Bowen Family Systems Theory and Practice: Illustration and Critique," 6.

13. Molly S. Castelloe, Ph.D., "How Trauma Is Carried Across Generations: Holding the secret history of our ancestors," https://www.psychologytoday.com/blog/the-me-in-we/201205/how-trauma-is-carried-across-generations.

Made in the USA
Coppell, TX
22 December 2023

26807672R00066